Prefa

My career in the heating industry
apprenticeship at the age of 17, this resulted in spending the
following decade as a service and repair engineer around the
Warrington and Manchester regions. A move to Australia
introduced me to the world of installing and repairing air
conditioning units, which I later learnt are called heat pumps if
you press a button on the controls. Fast forward a few years
and back in the UK I moved into teaching and training roles,
specifically as a heat pump technical training manager at Ideal
Heating and then teaching students the fundamentals of how
to become heating engineers as a lecturer of gas and
renewable energies at St Helens College.

It was whilst teaching at the college that I realised the modern
heating apprenticeship, much like the one I undertook myself,
teaches system design as if it's 1980. I had to educate myself
on modern heating system design over the years and
surprisingly I found it to be the most interesting thing I have
come across in my career to date. For me it has been
refreshing to see that over the past few years there has been
some fantastic content created that allows existing heating
engineers to learn more about the science of heating design
and specifically low temperature heating design. This inspired
me to utilise my experience of teaching students to help the
industry in my own little way, and explain the fundamentals of
low temperature heating design in a manner that those people
just starting out in their careers would understand. This then
progressed to me writing a version of this book in my spare
time and passing this onto my students so that they can refer
to it with their future installs. However, to my surprise, the
book gained some interest online and I subsequently received
messages from across the world asking could I publish and sell

copies of this book, so here is a (slightly) more professional version.

I do hope that any knowledge gained from this book is used in the manner it was intended. This is not a heat pump propaganda publication, nor is it implying that you are incompetent if you set the customer's boiler thermostat above 55°C. My primary goal in my career is to encourage more people into this industry and therefore I would like to make it a more welcoming place, especially on the education front. Coming from a similar economic background as many of the students I have taught, I am thankful that I fell into the profession as it has offered me so many opportunities already in my life and I would like to be able to help provide a chance for more young people to experience the same as I have.

Lewis Litherland

Contents

Introduction

I have written this book as a heating engineer intended to be read by heating engineers and hopefully, future heating engineers and I hope this comes across as such. Although the target audience I had in mind originally was heating apprentices, any engineer who is new to low temperature heating design will hopefully benefit from aspects of this publication.

This book will introduce the principles of how to design a modern central heating system without any bias towards heat pumps or gas boilers. Both heat pumps and condensing gas boilers work most efficiently at lower flow temperatures than what non-condensing boilers did and therefore much of this book is dedicated to teaching how this can be achieved whilst keeping the customer comfortable and happy with their system. From my own personal experience, the engineers of my generation and those that followed were slightly let down in their education on heating design and unfortunately were mostly taught the same principles as when installing a non-condensing boiler. I believe that part of my drive to write this book came from the feeling of having 'missed-out' on this key information myself early in my career and ensuring that the engineers of tomorrow do not experience the same.

When designing a heating system, it is very easy to get carried away with attempting to design every inch as efficiently as possible, but we must remember that at the end of the day it is the customer that will decide what they have installed and how they want to use it. Yes, efficiency should be one of the key focuses when designing a system but not the only consideration, every property and every customer is different and this must be factored in too, a great heating design is not just what looks good on paper.

Heat Loss Calculations

The first stage with any heating system design is to perform a room-by-room **Heat Loss calculation**. In simple terms, this tells the designer how much heat is required to be delivered into that room to achieve a specific **design internal temperature**.

As an example, all post-2006 well-insulated buildings should use an internal design temperature of **21°C in each room** apart from a **Bathroom *(22 °C)*** so the emitter in that room should be capable of heating the space to achieve the **desired internal temperature**. If a customer is vulnerable or infirm, then a higher design temperature of 23°C is recommended.

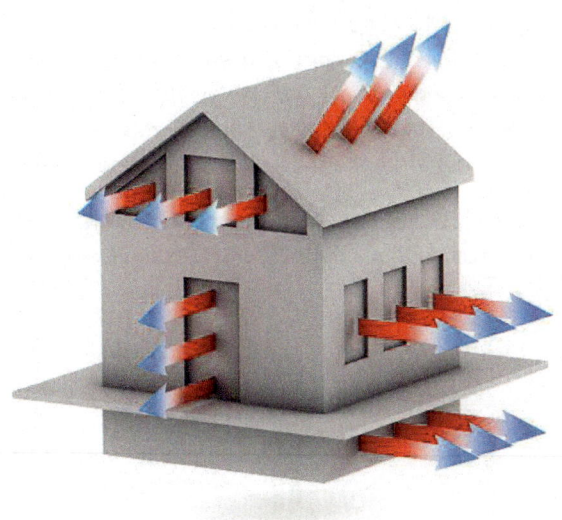

Heat Transfer

Technically, heat cannot be 'lost', it is just a form **energy** so is only ever transferred. It is never created or destroyed (this is what is known as the first law of **thermodynamics** within science) in the case of 'heat loss' from a property this is the **thermal energy** from within a dwelling being transferred to the outside air if its colder outside than inside.

It is scientifically impossible to prevent thermal energy being transferred from a warmer space to a cooler one. However, we can slow the rate of this transfer down by increasing the insulating properties of the substances we use to build properties.

As heat loss is a measure of energy transfer over time, we measure this in **Watts.**

A typical human body, at rest, can emit 100 Watts of thermal heat energy. So, if 10 people were in a space and that particular space had a 500-Watt heat loss this would mean that the space would begin to feel 'warmer' as the heat radiated from the bodies would be 1 Kilowatt and therefore greater than the heat 'lost' from the space. We call this **Heat Gain**.

There are other natural occurrences of heat gain, the most common of which within a building is **Solar Gain** from the sun.

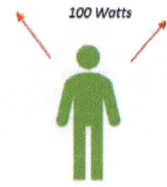

100 Watts

Calculating Heat Loss in a Dwelling

There are two mechanisms in which heat can be 'lost' from a property, these are through the **Fabric** of the building and through **Ventilation**.

Fabric Heat Loss

As the name would suggest, fabric heat loss is the conduction of heat through the **materials** that make up the fabric of the building, for example, brickwork, doors, windows etc. Each of these common building materials has something called a **U-Value.** Put simply, a U-value is the measure how effective a building material is in allowing heat energy to transfer through it. The lower the U-value number, the greater that material is as an insulator. So, for example, a brick wall would have a lower U-value than a glass window as the window would allow the heat to transfer through quicker than the brick. U-values can be found from various sources including the manufacturer of the product. Below is an example of the U-values for a PVCU-framed glass window.

PVCU-framed glass window	U-Value
Single Glazed	4.8
Double Glazed	2.8
Triple Glazed	2.1

Heat will only ever 'flow' to a space that is cooler (this is the second law of **thermodynamics**). This also means that the greater the difference in temperature between two areas the 'easier' that the heat will be transferred, this is why when it is colder outdoors our homes also become colder indoors. Within science the term **Delta T (ΔT)** is used when describing the **difference in temperature** between two points, for example if when calculating the fabric heat loss of an external wall, if the temperature in the lounge is 21°C and the temperature outdoors is -3°C then the Delta T between these two spaces would be 24°C. If a brick wall was separating the lounge from the outdoors in this scenario eventually the heat from the lounge would be transferred to the outdoors. Now, let's say the lounge is 21°C but it's a warmer day and the outdoor space is also 21°C, using the second law of thermodynamics, there would be no transfer of heat energy in this scenario and both areas would theoretically remain at the same temperature.

Now, the final piece of information we need to calculate fabric heat loss once we have the **U-value** and the **Delta T** is the **Area** of the building material itself, e.g. a brick wall that is 5 metres wide by 2.5 metres tall would have an area of 12.5m².

We now simply multiple these units by one another:

$$\textit{Fabric Heat Loss} = A \times U \times \Delta T$$

(Area x U Value x Difference in Temperature)

Ventilation Heat Loss

Ventilation heat loss refers to the amount of heat energy that is transferred through the **air** itself rather than through any materials. As a rule of thumb older homes have more **air changes** than a modern home, this is usually through air vents, cracks in the building structure, chimneys and the like. Also, certain rooms within a home have more air changes than others, such as a kitchen would have a large amount of air changes due to extractor fans operating or windows being opened when cooking etc. These values can be found from various resources. Below are a few examples of how the age of the property and type of room affect the air change per hour. It must be noted that some 'older' properties have significantly reduced their air changes over the years and an engineer should factor this into their design if so.

Room Type	Age of Room	Air Change per hour
Lounge	Pre 2000	1.5
Lounge	Post 2006	0.5
Bathroom	Pre 2000	3
Kitchen	Pre 2000	2

As with fabric heat loss we will need to factor in the **difference in temperature.** However, with ventilation heat loss, this is not a difference between adjoining rooms it is simply the difference between the outdoor design temperature and the internal design temperature. For example, if the outside/external design temperature was -2°C and the internal design temperature was 22°C then the Delta T would be 24°C.

As we have now found the air changes and temperature difference in our rooms, the next piece of data we need is the **volume** of the room. This is different from the fabric heat loss that only wants us to find the area of the material because obviously the room is filled by the air and so it is the volume that we calculate for ventilation heat loss. For example, a room that was 6 metres wide by 6 metres long and was 2.4 metres high would give a room volume of 86.4m^3 (6 x 6 x 2.4)

Now the final part we need to add into our equation is the **heat capacity of air**. For this calculation this is a given number of **0.33** (it is an approximation under normal conditions within a home). Heat capacities will be explained further into this book on page 62.

Ventilation Heat Loss = 0.33 x V x N x ΔT

(0.33 x Volume of Room x Number of Air Changes x Difference in temperature)

Total Room Heat Loss

So now that we have calculated the **fabric heat loss** within a room and the **ventilation heat loss** within a room, to find the total heat loss we simply **add these two numbers together.** This value allows us to select a suitable size emitter for that room to 'overcome' the heat loss. By adding all of the heat loss values in each room together we can then select a suitable size heating appliance. Then a suitable flow temperature to the emitters, system layout, controls to be used and all of the other aspects of designing a heating system.

Design Temperatures

Internal Design Temperature

As mentioned previously the internal design temperature for a modern property (post 2006) is recommended to be **21°C** in all rooms except a bathroom which should be **22°C**, again, these can be slightly altered to suit the customer's needs. For any property built prior to 2006 a different internal design temperature for each room was advised dependent on what this space was to be used for, e.g. a lounge would be 21°C whereas a bedroom would be designed for 18°C. An example of a few specific rooms can be found in the table below for reference. With this method of varying design temperatures heat loss and gains between rooms becomes a factor that an engineer must consider when designing a system. A higher heat loss in one room due to having a higher temperature than a neighbouring space may result in needing higher flow temperature, which can be detrimental to efficiency.

Room Type	Design Internal temp (pre-2006)
Lounge	21°C
Kitchen	18°C
Bedroom	18°C
Dining Room	21°C
Hall	18°C
Utility	18°C

External Design Temperature

The external design temperature that engineers work to varies upon where the property is situated in the country. Despite its small size the UK experiences different weather patterns in different areas, think about the difference between northern Scotland and Cornwall. There are various guides available to gain this data, but these can again be slightly altered to meet the customers individual needs and requirements. Below are a few examples of how this temperature varies upon location.

Location	External Design Temperature
London	-1.8°C
Birmingham	-3.4°C
Manchester	-2.2°C
Glasgow	-3.9°C

The Oversizing 'Problem'

The external design temperature given is, as you can see in the chart above, very low. Although it is possible to experience temperatures this low in the winter and even possibly even lower it is not often -4°C for 6 months of the year. So, if we design our heating system based on this low design temperature then we have a potential problem in that the heating system is **oversized** for a large part of the 'heating season'. Now why is oversizing a problem? Because it causes the heating appliance to **cycle**.

Cycling is when the heat source temperature turns on and off repeatedly. Think of it like this, we have a 5kW total heat loss in a property when it is -4°C outside, so we fit a system capable of heating this property. However, on this given example day, the outside temperature is actually 5°C, so now let's assume that the total heat loss in the property has now dropped to 3kW (due to the higher external temperature). The appliance gets a demand to fire up and heats up the system under the impression that it still needs to throw out 5kW worth of heat, so after a period the appliance reaches it's maximum temperature and turns itself off to cool down. The system now also cools and so does the property, then the appliance kicks back in again to compensate for this cooling down and the pattern repeats.

Why is this cycling behaviour a problem? Well for all heating appliances this means that multiple parts inside the appliance are having to stop and start repeatedly which puts undue stress on the components and leads to an increased risk in failure.

With **Heat Pumps** cycling has an even greater negative effect. Some heat pumps can draw **three times more** than their 'usual' electrical power upon start-up, this therefore means the efficiency of the appliance decreases significantly and the customer will unfortunately notice this on their monthly bills. If there is one key point that an engineer designing a system for a heat pump must have in their mind throughout, it is that **cycling must be kept to a minimum** in order to achieve a better efficiency.

Heating Controls

Heating controls are a means of controlling the amount of heat that is sent from the appliance to the system. Although they look like they do a similar job on the surface some controls still utilise an old-fashioned method of setting a target room temperature and then once this is met, they stop the appliance completely. We call these **on/off stats**. The idea of an/off stat is simple, the numbers on the front read the ambient room temperature, the customer sets their desired target temperature and the heating appliance turns on, heats the room until this target is met, the customer hears a 'click' and exactly like a light switch the power demand is cut off and so the heating appliance turns off. After a period of no heat entering the room, the temperature will fall below the target again and the process repeats. You can see that is causing **cycling**.

On/off stats were created over 100 years ago and had their place when appliances could not modulate their heat output. As described earlier if the system had been designed to heat a room up to 21°C when it was -3°C outside and had a 10kW heat loss then too much heat would be sent into the system if it was actually a 10°C external temperature on that day and only now had a 4.5kW heat loss.

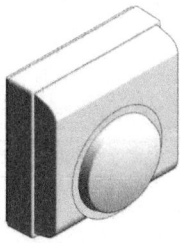

Welcome to the Modern World?

Look at your mobile phone and think about the phone you had 5 years ago, now think about the phone you had 10 years ago. Do the same with your TV, your computer. You will realise that technology has progressed rapidly in just a few short years, so isn't it strange that on/off thermostats created 100 years ago are still being installed today? Yes, they do their job but there are much, much more efficient controls on the market and have been for a while now. The one heating control that should really be installed on most heating systems today to increase efficiency is weather compensation.

Weather Compensation

Weather Compensation is not a new technology, it has been around certain parts of the industry for a number of years. The principle of it is this, a sensor reads the external/outdoor temperature and automatically adjusts the kW of the appliance accordingly by adjusting the temperature the water is heated to within the appliance. It is a simple idea, if a system has been designed to send **8kW** of heat into the property when it is **-4°C** outside then if it is actually only **5°C** outside it only sends out **5kW** of heat. This has a magnitude of benefits for the appliance, the system, the customer and the environment.

Weather compensation controls are usually a small device that is externally mounted and then wired directly to the heating appliance, some are also installed physically onto the appliance such as with an air source heat pump and some simply use the internet to send weather data to the appliance.

Below is an example of the **'curves'** that an engineer could set within an air source heat pumps controls, you can see how the outdoor temperature has a direct effect on the flow temperature of the appliance.

As an example, if the engineer chose a curve of '*0.75*' on their appliance, if the outdoor temperature was -10°C then the flow temperature would be roughly 40°C. Whereas if the external temperature was 5°C, the flow temperature would be roughly 33°C.

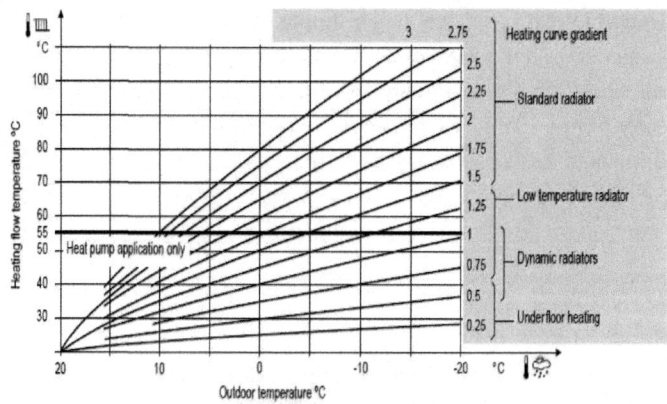

Load Compensation

Load Compensation controls perform a similar role to weather compensation controls however their main difference is that instead of reading the outside air temperature like a weather comp' control, they read the **internal room temperature** instead and modulate the flow temperature out of the appliance accordingly.

Although this type of control sits within the property and reads the temperature, it is vital to emphasise that a load compensation controller does not work the same as an on/off thermostat.

Weather compensation with Load compensation?

There is no one size fits all for anything within this industry, there are too many variables, the most common being how different properties are to each other and how different customers are to each other. As a guide, a **highly insulated** property that has **high solar gains** and retains heat 'well' would benefit more from some form of **load compensation** as the external temperature won't have as high an influence on the internal temperature as it would in a lesser insulated property. When weather compensation and load compensation are both installed on a system the amount of **influence** the room temperature has on the flow temperature over the external temperature can be adjusted by the installer or customer to suit.

Heating Appliances

Delta-T

When designing heating systems, we must decide what the
difference in temperature between the return into the
appliance and the flow out of it once heated will be (**ΔT**). In
simple terms – how much are we going to heat the water up by
when it gets back to the appliance.

Key Point: This is *mainly* affected by **Pipe Work Size** (diameter)
and the **Pump Speed.**

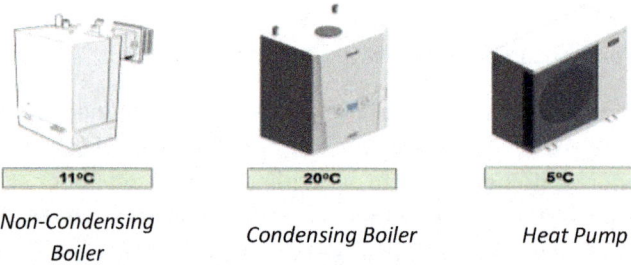

| 11°C | 20°C | 5°C |

*Non-Condensing
Boiler*   *Condensing Boiler*   *Heat Pump*

These recommended Delta-T's above help to provide the best
efficiency for the individual appliance and the reasons for this
will be discussed in the coming pages. It is vitally important
that when replacing one 'type' of appliance for another that
the system is designed to enable the appliance to achieve as
close as possible these recommended Delta-T's.

A **Non-Condensing Boiler** was designed to be attached to a system that has a DT of around **11°C**. The reason for this is because if the return temperature entering the boiler was 'low' (below 55°C) when it entered the appliance the hot emission gases would then **condense onto the heat exchanger**. The materials these appliances were made from would corrode and rust and reduce the lifespan of the boiler.

A **Condensing Boiler** is designed to be attached to a system that has a DT of around **20°C**. With these appliances we want to achieve as low a return temperature as possible in order to extract as much heat as we can from the flue gases (this will be explained in more detail on the next page). If the return temperature is below 55°C then condensation will occur on the heat exchanger as a by-product. However, the **Stainless steel** or **Aluminum** construction will not rust with this condensation.

Condensing Boilers

The Temperature at which **condensing** occurs in a boiler is when the **return** water temperature is around **54°C.** The science behind this specific number is that although the burner will produce a flame that is around **900°C** by the time this heat is transferred through the heat exchanger it has cooled to around **65°C.** As heat will always be attracted to something cooler (think a cold ice cube in a drink) then the *hotter* flue gases will transfer their heat energy to the *cooler* return water, so if we position this return water at the point furthest from the flame, such as at the bottom of a rectangular heat exchanger or the outer 'ring' of a cylindrical heat exchanger we will therefore transfer some of this flue gas heat into our system rather than it being lost out of the flue to warm up the garden. When this happens condensation is formed, in the same way that when you breathe your 'warm' breath onto a cool window condensation occurs.

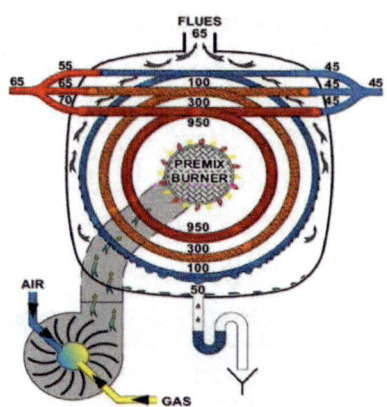

Below is an extract from a gas boilers' manufacturer's instructions. It is interesting to note that when you **lower the temperature** the appliance is producing, we can actually attain a higher **kW output**.

This is all down to extracting more heat from the flue gases. **The lower the temperature – the higher the efficiency of our appliance.**

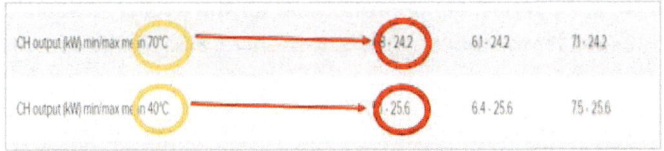

This graph below shows the relationship between **boiler efficiency** and **return water temperature**. As you can see the **Dew Point** at **54°C** is not the maximum efficiency level of the boiler but is the point when condensation begins to occur.

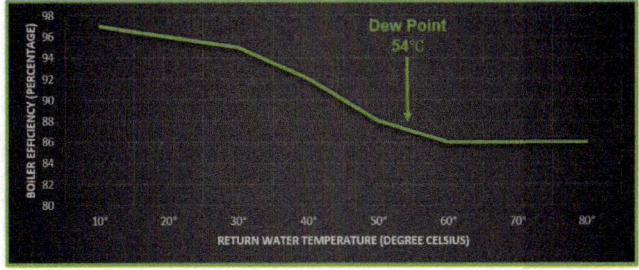

At this point it is vitally important to state that **Appliance Efficiency** and **System Efficiency** are two different things. However, system efficiency obviously has a huge effect on the appliance efficiency.

Manufacturers of gas boilers must ensure that a new condensing boiler is capable of achieving **92% efficiency** (ErP) however as you can see from the graph on the previous page, if you were to install this brand-new boiler onto a system that allowed the return temperature to enter the appliance at 65°C for example, this boiler would now only be 86% efficient not 92%.

A research study conducted in 2009 by the Energy Savings Trust found that the mean efficiency of a trial set of *regular* boilers was **85.3%** with a standard deviation of 2.5% and that the mean efficiency of a trial set of combination boilers was **82.5%** with a standard deviation of 4.0%.

Why the lack of efficiency?

Using the knowledge that a high return temperature lowers the efficiency of a condensing boiler, to discover why some of these boilers are not as efficient as they could/should be we must look at the most common reasons as to why a return temperature would be high.

High Flow Temperatures

Even with a correct DT of 20°C a boiler that has a flow temperature set to 80°C would not condense as the return temperature would still be above the **Dew Point**. We will discuss the recent changes to part L of the building regulations that has been brought about to alleviate this on page 45.

It must be noted that reducing the flow temperature will reduce the mean water temperature of the emitters and therefore these emitters will require a larger surface area. However, in properties that still have an older heating system installed but the heat loss has been reduced over the years due to installing double glazed windows and insulation then these radiators may already be at a suitable size to run at lower temperatures.

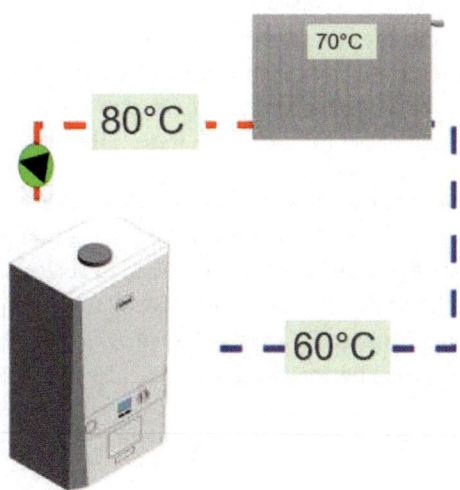

Incorrect System Design

An incorrect (narrow) Delta T is the most common cause for a modern condensing boiler to not be as efficient as it could/should be. There are multiple reasons that can cause the DT to be narrower than it should, such as the pipe size is too large and that the pump speed is set too high on systems. This therefore means that the water is flowing out of the boiler and returning back quicker than it should be and the consequence of this is that the heat energy does not have the time to transfer from the system into the surroundings.

'Fast' Boiler Swaps – The Issues

A gas engineer replacing a non-condensing boiler with a new condensing boiler will need to assess if whether the existing heating pipework is adequately sized to accommodate a condensing boiler. As discussed, the Delta-T of a non-condensing boiler differs from that of a condensing boiler, so if a system was designed to work with a 11°C DT simply taking this boiler off the wall and replacing it with a 'condensing' boiler will not affect the Delta-T in most appliances.

Some more intelligent modern boilers may have a control board that can 'talk' to the integral circulating pump and attempt to rectify an incorrect Delta-T themselves but there is a limit to the amount of correction these boilers can achieve and of course, designing a system correctly in the first instance will always give a better efficiency.

A non-condensing-condensing boiler

As shown in the images below, the condensing boiler that has been installed onto this system will not condense (apart from on startup) if the boiler thermostat was set to 70°C and no weather compensation controls were fitted as the return temperature is at a higher temperature than the 54°C dew point temperature.

A 'boiler swap' job will need to include a full system design calculation and pipework alterations are often necessary to ensure that a condensing boiler is officially a condensing boiler.

The process of how to correctly size pipework, components and the setting of a circulating pump for the best efficiency are covered later in this book from pages 43 onwards.

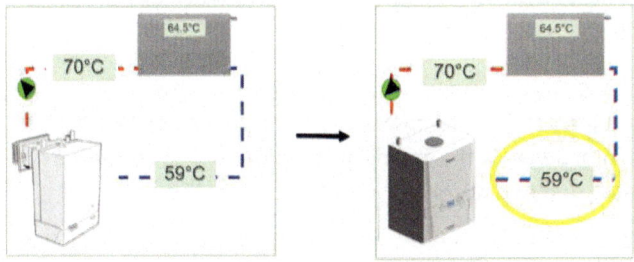

'Creating' Heat Within Appliances

Natural Gas Boilers

The **flue** of a natural gas boiler has two sections, an **inner and outer** flue.

Although these two are housed within one component they are kept separate from each other as they perform differing jobs.

Air is dragged in through the **outer-flue** and into the boiler from outside of the property. This air is then mixed with a gas primarily made up of methane, the mixture of natural gas and air is then ignited, and a controlled 'fire' is started at a component aptly named the **burner**. This thermal energy is then transferred into the **heat exchanger** and subsequently heated water is pumped around the heating system before returning back to the heat exchanger ready to start the cycle again.

The inner-flue is under **positive pressure** and it's job is to dispel the **products of combustion** to a safe place (e.g. to outside). Below is the chemical equation for the **complete** combustion of natural gas.

$$CH_4 + 2O_2 = CO_2 + 2H_2O + HEAT$$

(Methane + Oxygen = Carbon Dioxide + Water Vapour + Heat)

Now, that is the formula for *complete* combustion, however it is important to note that in reality the air entering the gas boiler will never be pure oxygen and as such the level will be decreased, this therefore means that **Carbon Monoxide (CO)** is also produced which can be fatal to humans and hence the reason for the flue needing to terminate outside of a property for safety reasons.

We have two negatives when creating heat from a natural gas boiler, one is that **Carbon Dioxide** is expelled into the atmosphere and secondly, we will always **'lose' heat** through the flue to outside the property, so a natural gas boiler will never reach 100% efficiency.

What is Efficiency?

Efficiency with a heating appliance is easily described as; How much heat are you putting into the heating system compared to how much energy you are putting into the appliance to create this heat.

If I placed 10 'lots' of natural gas into my boiler and only received 9 'lots' of heat into my radiators from this then my boiler would be 90% efficient.

However, with heating appliances efficiency and running costs are two separate matters. They have a direct relationship with one and other yes, but running costs are based upon how much is the consumer **paying** for this energy. A boiler running at 98% efficiency for a total of 18 hours a day may actually be costing the customer more than an 80% efficient boiler running for 5 hours a day.

Heat Pumps

Much like a gas boiler, a heat pumps role is to produce heat for a heating and/or hot water system. The process of 'creating' this heat is slightly different however and enables a potentially **higher efficiency rating** (as stated previously this doesn't necessarily equal lower running costs) and has **zero Carbon Dioxide** emissions at the point of use.

Heat pumps come in many varieties and layouts, but all perform the same role; they extract heat from a source, this can be the air, ground, water to name a few, and then manipulate this heat in a way that makes it 'useful' to warm our spaces and hot water systems.

The image below is of an air-source heat pump and would be placed outside of a property so that it extracts heat energy from the outside air. It's of interest to note that even on a cold winters day in the UK there is a great deal of **heat energy in the air** still, in fact you would have to get right down to **-273°C (named absolute zero)** for there to be zero 'heat' in the air and you probably wouldn't be worrying about your heat pump working at that stage. However, in truth air source heat pumps do have a minimum temperature that they can work down to, but this can be around -20°C for most manufacturers.

The Vapour Compression Cycle

If you hadn't realised already, there has been quite a few scientific explanations dropped in within this book so far. In the original version, I had dedicated the first three pages all to thermodynamics and the key scientific principles that an engineer would need to understand to help them with their day to day work, but I then assumed that most people wouldn't read any further beyond this out of boredom so I have instead been drip feeding them in. Here's some vital science that is needed to understand how a heat pump operates and it is relating to two laws, **Charles** and **Boyles Laws**.

- **Charles Law** in straight forward talk = By reducing the amount of space (volume) that a gas occupies, the temperature increases. An easy example is this, when you pump up a football with a hand pump it gets hot because you are compressing the air within. In a little deeper science, think of the gas molecules suddenly having less space to float around and then all crashing into one another, this creates heat. Of course, the opposite of this is also true, if you increase the volume of the space, the temperature now decreases, think of a deodorant can becoming colder as you hold the nozzle down.

- **Boyles Law** in straight forward talk = By reducing the amount of space (volume) that a gas occupies, the pressure increases.

- **Key point**: If we can manipulate the pressure of a gas, we can also manipulate it's temperature.

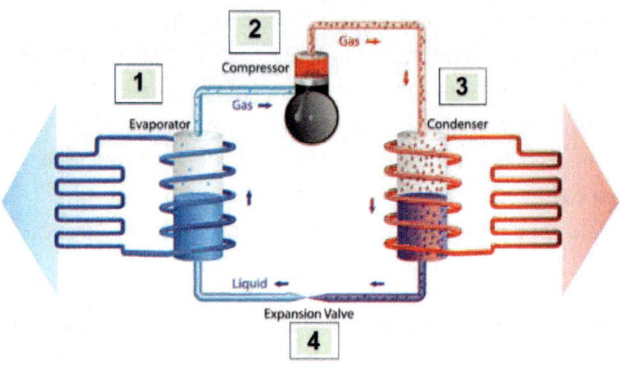

The image above is a basic version of how the **vapour compression cycle** works within a heat pump. The cycle is also sometimes referred to as the **refrigeration cycle** as the substance that is moving through the cycle isn't water but a **refrigerant**. Explaining refrigerants in detail would take up a whole book so the key point that we need to know with refrigerants for heating design purposes is that they have a **low boiling point.** Water obviously has a boiling point of 100°C, although the phrase most people miss after this statement is "at atmospheric pressure". You may have already heard that at the top of Mount Everest water actually boils at around 70°C as it has **less pressure** up there due to the altitude.

Most common refrigerants in heat pumps boil from a liquid into a gas at around **-40°C** or **-50°C** at **atmospheric pressure**.

Key point: By **altering the pressure** of the refrigerant we can allow it to change state when we want it to (from a liquid to gas or vice-versa)

We will start with the **Evaporator.** As the name suggests this is the component where a liquid refrigerant evaporates and turns into a gas. On an air source heat pump the evaporator is the little pipe coils that have fins attached that usually sit behind the fan. When the fan spins it drags air and therefore heat across the coils and by this very slight increase in temperature allows it to extract the heat from the air into the refrigerant and this then evaporates into a gas.

The **Compressor** then sucks this gaseous state refrigerant in and compresses it. As mentioned previously if you reduce the volume a gas occupies then you increase its temperature and pressure, so this now hot and highly pressured gas leaves the compressor.

This is then directed into the **Condenser**. The reason the refrigerant condenses here is the same reason that the flue gases within a condensing boiler condense, the hot refrigerant gas cools down as it transfers its heat into the heating system. On the majority of heat pumps this is simply done in a plate heat exchanger, one side is refrigerant and on the other side is the water within the heating system.

Finally, the refrigerant enters the **Expansion Valve**, and expands - as mentioned on a previous page if the volume increases, the temperature of the substance decreases. We need the refrigerant to be really cool now as it will need to be cooler than the outside air temperature in order to extract its heat in the evaporator (remember heat only moves to a cooler substance).

Heat Pump Delta-T

The design Delta-T of a heat pump should ideally be around **5°C** for optimum efficiency of the vapour compression cycle and therefore of the heating system. We will discuss the relationship between flow rates and temperature differences in more detail later in the book but in essence, the narrower the Delta-T, the greater the flow rate and vice-versa. In simple terms, the water moving around a system attached to a heat pump would need to be flowing quicker than if a gas boiler was the chosen heating appliance.

Gas boiler to heat pump retrofits

A common misconception when installing a heat pump on an 'older property' when replacing a gas boiler is that all of the pipework is too small and so must be replaced. As we know, non-condensing boilers were designed to run on DT 11. This pipework could have/probably was, installed back in the days before cavity wall insulation, double glazing and other insulating improvements. So, when replacing single for double glazing the heat loss in that property would have reduced, did the window fitter then rip out the pipework and reduce its size? Or take out the radiator and replace with a smaller one? probably not. This means that in most older homes the pipework and radiators are probably already oversized and therefore very little work will need to be done if replacing a gas boiler for a heat pump and getting from DT11 to DT5.

Heat pump efficiency

Heat pump efficiency is measured the same as gas boiler efficiency but is called by a different name and stated as a number rather than as a percentage. A heat pump's efficiency is measured in it's Coefficient of Performance (**COP**) or by its Seasonal Coefficient of Performance (**SCOP**). To put this simply, COP is a snapshot in time whereas SCOP is the average annually and therefore is more useful. A COP or SCOP of, for example 4, basically means that the heat pump is running at 400% efficiency.

It's a strange concept that an appliance can be more than 100% efficient but this is all down to how a heat pump extracts the heat from its source. The compressor is the part that uses the most energy (electricity) in a heat pump but the amount of energy that is absorbed from the source (air, ground etc') is technically 'free' so to speak. A heat pump could use one 'lot' of electricity to power the compressor and the other electrical components but then extract 3 lots of energy from the source, this would therefore mean that the appliance is 400% efficient as it can now deliver 4 'lots' of heat into the property but has only used 1 'lot' of electricity.

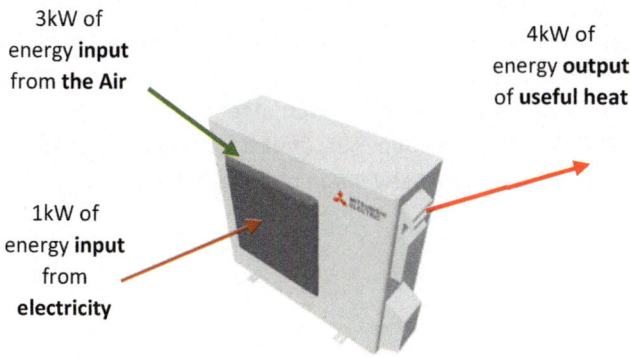

3kW of energy **input** from **the Air**

4kW of energy **output** of **useful heat**

1kW of energy **input** from **electricity**

External Temperature and COP

The reason that SCOP is a more useful piece of information than COP is due to the effect that the external temperature has on the efficiency of an air source heat pump. Unlike a gas boiler, the efficiency could change more dramatically day to day or even hour to hour based on the temperature outside. A ground source heat pump isn't affected as much by the external temperature as the ground has a similar temperature year-round once you reach around 15metres down.

A well-designed air source heat pump's heating system would still perform its role perfectly fine on a cold day as mentioned previously there is always heat energy in the air, however the amount of **work** the compressor needs to undertake on a colder day would be greater than on a warmer day. Logically, the colder the outside temperature the less heat energy can be extracted from the air, so the more work the compressor would have to do, meaning more electricity is used.

External Temperature and Maximum kW Output

An engineer designing a system would need to consider that an air source heat pump's maximum kW rating would also be affected by the outside air temperature. A 10kW unit may only have a maximum of 10kW heat output when the external temperature is 7°C but if the external temperature was to drop to -7°C then the maximum output of the appliance may drop to 8.5kW (this varies between manufacturers).

Heating System Layouts

The problem with S and Y Plans

S and Y plan systems have been around for over half a century and are the two most common layouts of central heating systems in the UK, apart from the combination boiler. However, they have one vital flaw and that is that they cannot inform the appliance of whether there is a hot water demand or a central heating demand. The orange wire within a 2 port or 3 port valve is tasked with sending power to the pump and boiler and informing them to 'start'. In an S-plan system the orange wire from the heating zone valve and the orange wire from the hot water zone valve are joined together so the pump and the boiler have no idea what demand has been asked, they just know that they need to fire up ASAP. Now why is this a problem for efficiency? As an S or Y plan system will have a hot water cylinder, the flow temperature from the appliance will commonly need to be set higher than 50/60°C to achieve a domestic hot water temperature of 50/60°C within the cylinder. So, if this is the case then the appliance will 'fire' at a high temperature regardless of if there is only a central heating demand as it cannot differentiate between the type of demand. To ensure that **compensation controls** work as intended, then the appliance will need to recognise the type of demand and therefore be capable of producing two differing flow temperatures- a **higher temperature** for a **hot water** demand and a (typically) **lower temperature** controlled by compensation controls for a **heating** demand.

Priority Domestic Hot Water Systems

The alternative to an S or Y plan is to treat the system in the same way that a combination boiler works, with **priority domestic hot water**.

These systems cannot provide both central heating and hot water simultaneously but with the development in high-gain cylinders, the fact that the full output of the appliance is sent to the cylinder coil and the minimum heat loss of these cylinders the recovery times would be so short that it would not be detrimental to the system user if designed correctly.

Another advantage of a system utilising PDHW is that the appliance chosen would only be sized to deliver the output of either the central heating or the hot water and not both simultaneously. The largest demand is the one that will determine the kW output, so this would mean that the customer would most likely be purchasing a cheaper appliance due to the lower kW output.

A pre-plumbed heat pump cylinder is likely to arrive piped and wired in a PDHW configuration offering a simple 'plug and play' option for installers.

D Plan and X Plan Systems

With a PDHW system there is still a choice of system layouts as there is with a traditional S or Y plan. The industry has begun to refer to these as **D plan** and **X plan** systems.

D Plan System Layout

A D plan system looks from the outside like a traditional **Y plan system** where somebody has mistakenly placed the 3-port the wrong way around. (The B port is now facing heating and the A port is facing Hot Water). This type of system ensures that central heating is the 'default' setting for the valve (it rests in CH). Therefore, if a heating demand is placed, the appliance fires using **compensation** controls only and the valve does not receive a signal to change position.

D Plan System Wiring

Wiring a D Plan system is a very simple task, the grey wire and the white wire from the valve are joined together. This means that when a hot water demand is placed the valve will now open. As the valve 'rests' in central heating position, a 'loss' of demand ensures the valve sits back to central heating and compensation controls modulate the appliance flow temperature. The neutral and earth (if required) are both terminated as they 'usually' would be on an S and Y plan.

X Plan System Layout

As much as a D plan System looks like a traditional Y plan system, the X plan looks similar to an **S plan** system. The only difference with the physical layout of the X-plan is that the central heating zone valve is a **normally open valve** as opposed to a normally closed valve as it would be in an S-plan.

This means that the central heating can work off compensation controls without a signal being sent to a zone valve (as it is 'resting' open).

Wiring an X Plan System

The wiring for an X-plan system is simple. The **brown wires** from both the heating zone valve and the hot water zone valve are terminated together, this therefore means that when the normally closed hot water zone valve receives a signal to open up the normally open central heating zone valve receives a signal to close and of course when the hot water demand is satisfied the central heating zone valve opens again as the hot water valve closes.

*Simply 'join' the brown
wires together.*

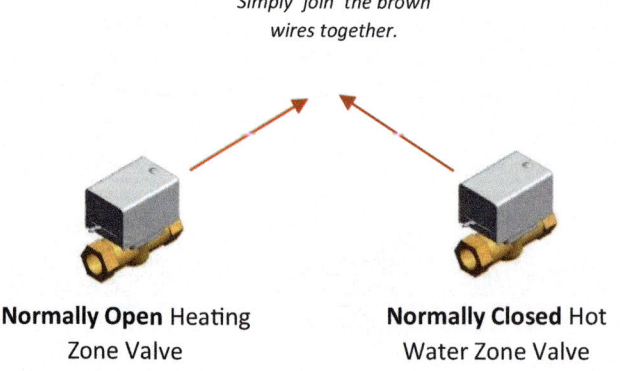

Normally Open Heating
Zone Valve

Normally Closed Hot
Water Zone Valve

Stored Hot Water Systems

As with all other aspects of the industry, the technology used within stored hot water systems has improved so much over the last half a century that the systems installed today are almost unrecognisable to the early days. Unvented cylinders capable of supplying 3 bar worth of pressure have replaced gravity-fed systems. Also the days of a 'duvet' insulation jacket loosely thrown over a small copper cylinder have long been replaced with the latest insulation-covered cylinders with very little standing heat losses. Thermostats used to monitor the temperatures within the cylinders have also been updated drastically to give a more accurate control. One major improvement has been the coils used within indirect cylinders, technological advances have brought about larger surface areas and innovate designs of these coils to decrease the amount of time it takes to heat the water to a target temperature (the reheat time).

Sizing a Domestic HW Cylinder

There are two main considerations when determining the size of a hot water cylinder to install within a property: the required volume for the household and the capabilities of the heat source. The first point in regards to the required volume, is that the cylinder should be sized mainly according to the property itself and not the number of current occupants at the time of design (the number of people physically living in a house is likely to change over the years).

BS6700 states that an allowance of 45 litres-per person is a reasonable and quick method of calculating the volume required for a stored hot water cylinder. This guidance also assumes that 2 people are sharing the main bedroom, so for example in a 3-bedroom property the calculation would be 45litres x 4 people = 180 litres required.

There are many reference guides available from manufactures to refer to that take into account the number of bathrooms and en-suites that a property has and also the maximum rated heat output of the heat source. For example, a 4 bedroom property with one bathroom, one en-suite and a heat source with a maximum rated output at 6kW would require 250 litres worth of volume.

Hot Water Calculations

It is possible for an engineer to calculate the reheat times of the cylinder in relation to its volume to determine the requirements for that system, property and customer. This is achieved via use of the equation below.

$$\text{Reheat Time (mins)} = \frac{\text{Volume (litres)} \times (T_2 - T_1)}{14.3 \times kW}$$

Breaking down the equation

T_2 represents the **target** water temperature, whereas T_1 is the **actual** water temperature.

14.3 is a 'given' for this equation and represents 60 seconds divided by the specific heat capacity of water (4.2kj/L/K). The specific heat capacity is the amount of energy that is required to raise the temperature of a substance by 1°C, this is covered in more detail later in the book.

The **kW** is the value that is **lowest** out of either the heat output of the heating appliance or the rating of the coil within the cylinder.

As an example, we will state that we have a 170litre cylinder connected to a 10kW heat pump with a 12kW rated cylinder coil and we need to heat the water within the cylinder from 35°C to 55°C.

$$\frac{170 \text{ litres} \times 20°C}{14.3 \times 10kW} \longrightarrow \frac{3400}{143}$$

= 24 mins

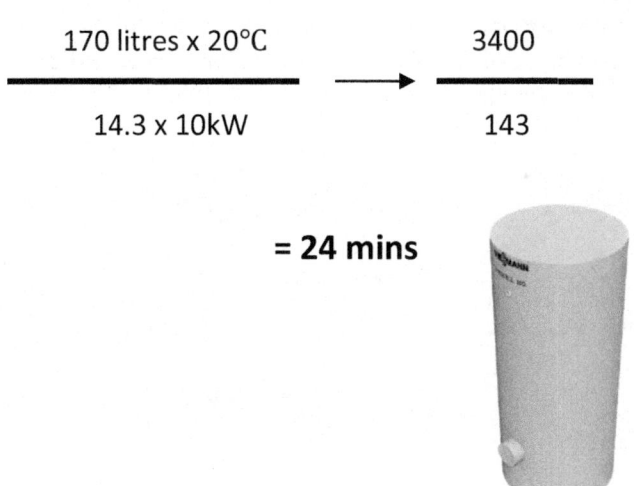

As with most equations, the units to calculate the reheat time can be rearranged to provide the engineer with other important information.

If the engineer would like to state to the customer the minimum size of heat input that is required to reheat their cylinder within a certain time, then the equation will be rearranged to resemble the following.

$$kW = \frac{\text{Volume (litres)} \times (T_2 - T_1)}{14.3 \times \text{Reheat Time (mins)}}$$

Therefore, as our next example, if the reheat time on a 210litre cylinder from 30°C up to 55°C would like to be within 20 minutes, we would need the heating appliance and the coil to both to be capable of giving at least 18.35kW output. The 'working out' for this is shown below.

170litres x 25°C = 5250

14.3 x 20mins = 286

5250 ÷ 286 = **18.35kW**

Pumps (Circulators)

Early pumps commonly had 3 speed settings, these are called **fixed speed pumps.** No matter what happened with the system this pump would still spin at a pre-determined speed set by the installer. In a way it had no idea what was happening around it, its job was just to circulate when given power.

If a customer suddenly turned 4 of their 6 radiators off it made no difference at all to this pump's speed.

A Circulating pump will be identified first by its internal diameter orifice and then by its maximum head of 'power'. For example, this Grundfos **15/50** to the left is named as it has a 15mm internal diameter and a maximum of a 5 metre head delivery.

This Grundfos Alpha 1L 15/60 pump can be placed in a variety of modes from the basic fixed speed to variable pressure, underfloor heating mode, radiator mode or PWM speed mode. This variety of settings allows this pump to potentially increase the efficiency of the system it is installed on to.

To the right is a **pump chart** for a
Wilo Para 6 metre head pump if set
in the **constant/fixed speed mode**.
The way to read this chart is as
follows; If the pump is set to speed 3
this would give 6 metres head of
pressure, speed 2 would give 4
metres head of pressure and speed 1
would give 2 metres head of
pressure.

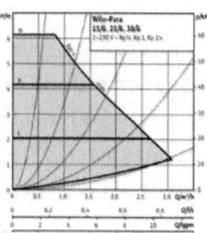

Now the image on the right shows
the same pump but in **variable
pressure mode**. As flow rate is the
horizontal axis and metres of head is
the vertical axis you can see that if
the resistance decreases then the
pump speed also decreases.

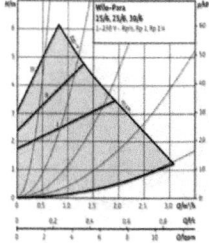

A **pulse width modulation pump**
(PWM) 'communicates' with the
heating appliance **directly** by getting
signals from components such as the
thermistors to either speed up or
slow down to try to maintain an
optimum flow rate within the
appliance.

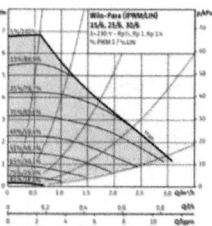

Radiator Sizing

The recent updates to **Part L** of the building regulations state that all **new** heating systems should be designed to a maximum **flow** temperature of **55°C** this is not just systems heated by a heat pump but also includes properties heated by a natural gas boiler too.

As we have previously mentioned, a low return temperature would increase the efficiency of a condensing boiler. So, by having a lower flow temperature this would automatically reduce the return temperature.

With heat pumps a low flow temperature is also vital to an efficient heating system, the **less work** the compressor must perform, the **more efficient** the heat pump.

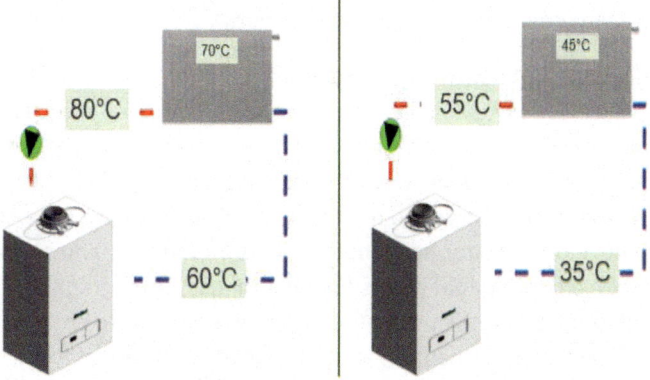

Heat and Temperature

Heat and temperature are two different things. In simple terms, **temperature** is how hot something is to **touch**, and **heat** is how much of this temperature then 'flows' or is '**transferred**'.

A straightforward way of explaining this is imagine a lighter, if you were to place a thermometer in the path of the flame of a lighter it would say that there may be 700°C worth of temperature in that flame. Now if that flame was the only source of heat in a 3 bed property, would it heat the home? No of course not, it is too small. The lighter has a high temperature but gives off little heat.

As this section is titled 'Radiator Sizing' you may have worked out where this is going. If we are to **lower the temperature** of our radiators to make our appliances as efficient as possible then we will need to **increase the size** of our radiators to allow them to emit enough **heat** into the room.

In theory we could install a radiator that covers an entire wall space in a lounge and create a mean water temperature of this radiator of 27°C and it would heat the room to a comfortable temperature, however it would probably look awful and so no customer would agree to this being installed. But if we were to remove the radiator from the wall, lie it on the floor and cover it with a flooring that allows the heat to 'pass through' then the room would still be heated by a low temperature emitter. This is **underfloor heating** and the reason it is a very efficient form of heating emitter, low temperature, large surface area.

Radiator Outputs

All radiator catalogues will state a kW that the emitter can produce along with its dimensions. However, this kW output is often given if the **flow temperature** into the radiator is **75**°C, the **return temperature** is **65**°C and **the target room** temperature is **20**°C. We call this **DT50**. (The UK has used this method since 2013)

DT50 =

(The Mean of 75°C and 65°C is 70°C. Then minus the 20°C room temp = 50°C)

But if we do not have the same temperatures as those stated in the catalogue (which we shouldn't if we are designing a low temperature system) then the kW of the radiator will not be what is stated once installed on our system, and we must therefore work out what size radiator we will actually require to achieve the kW we need to heat the space.

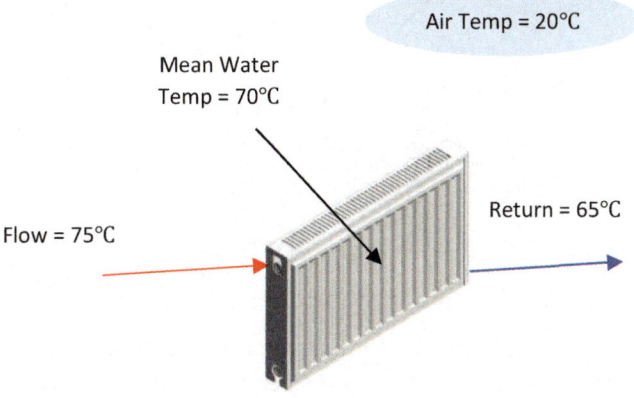

Air Temp = 20°C

Mean Water Temp = 70°C

Return = 65°C

Flow = 75°C

Correction Factor Calculation

We first need to determine the **difference** between the **mean water temperature** and **target air temperature** that we are to have in the system we are designing (MWT-AT).

For this example, we will set the flow temperature to 50°C and the return is 30°C. This would then give us a mean water temperature in our radiator of 40°C.

$$(50+30 = 80) / 2 = 40.$$

The target room temperature we will say is 21°C. So, our difference in temperature between the mean water temperature of the radiator and the air temperature is **19°C.** (40-21 = 19)

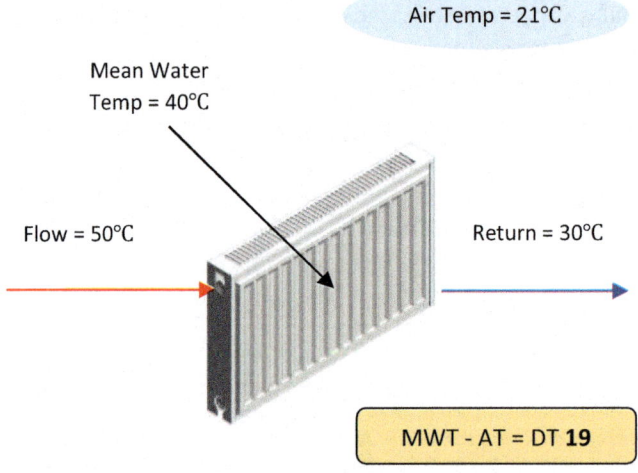

To now find the size of the radiator in the catalogue we actually need based off of the temperatures we have in our system we must calculate the **correction factor**.

The equation for this is;

$$(\text{Actual Delta T} \div \text{Catalogue Delta T})^{1.3}$$

So, in our example, our sum would be $(19 \div 50)^{1.3} = 0.284$

(Tip: if using a mobile phone as a calculator you may need to turn it horizontal to access the scientific buttons)

So, what does this correction factor tell us? And why is it useful for a heating engineer? Well, as the correction factor is **0.284**, the radiator from the catalogue will only output **28.4%** of its stated kW on our system.

So as an example, if the room heat loss was **900Watts** and we had a correction factor of 0.284 then the actual output of a 900Watts catalogue radiator would be **255.6Watts** so it would be too small.

$$(900 \times 0.284 = 255.6\text{Watts})$$

Now technically we can flip this equation on it's on head to tell us what size of radiator we need, if we were to **divide** the 900Watts by the correction factor then this would inform us of a radiator output we would need for *our* system.

$$(900\text{Watts} \div 0.284 = 3.17\text{kW})$$

Pipe Configuration Factor

Of course, as this is the heating industry there are more variables we must consider that would affect the output of the radiator in a property, the most common of which is how the radiator's pipework is configured.

New radiators arrive with 4 blank 'corners' and the engineer can technically choose how to connect this radiator onto the heating system's pipework. One connection at the top of the radiator must be used for a bleed vent (as air will always rise to the top) but the other connections can be in any order of choice.

In the UK the most common of these configurations is **bottom, bottom, opposite end (BBOE).** This is where the flow and return both connect at the bottom of the radiator at opposite ends. However, this is not how most radiator catalogues state their configuration, nor is it the most efficient way to pipe a radiator.

Most Radiator catalogues will state the kW of a radiator based on a **top, bottom, same end** (TBSE) configuration and just to confuse matters further, the most efficient configuration is actually **top, bottom, opposite ends** (TBOE).

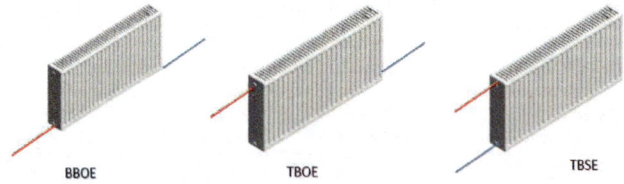

BBOE   TBOE   TBSE

As the radiator catalogue states their outputs as **TBSE** we will need another correction factor if we are to pipe the radiator differently to this.

(BBOE) Bottom, bottom, opposite ends = x 0.96

(TBOE) Top, bottom, opposite ends = x 1.05

As an example of how we combine these two correction factors to determine the actual output of our given radiator we will again use the heat loss of a room being 900Watts, the Delta T correction factor will be 0.284 again and we will pipe the radiator up as a BBOE.

900Watts ÷ (0.284 x 0.96) = 3.30kW

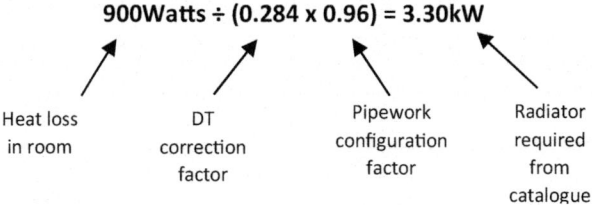

| Heat loss in room | DT correction factor | Pipework configuration factor | Radiator required from catalogue |

There are even more variables such as the paint that is applied the radiator, whether there is a shelf above, if it is in a recess and more, but for a heating engineer to choose an output of radiator these are the two most common variables that should be highlighted.

The Correction Factor 'Cheat Sheet'

As a heating engineer time is often of the essence. So thankfully we have a cheat sheet available for reference below.

This cheat sheet is for radiators that are piped up **BBOE** and from a catalogue stating a **DT of 50°C** (as most are in the UK) and all the engineer has to do is calculate is the Delta T between the meat water temperature and the air temperature (both Correction factors have already been calculated). Simply find the DT (round up If not a whole number) and multiply the room's heat loss by the correction factor to give you the actual radiator size you need in the catalogue.

Mean Water Temp to Air Temp DT (°C)	Correction Factor
15	4.98
16	4.58
17	4.23
18	3.93
19	3.66
20	3.43
21	3.22
22	3.03
23	2.86
24	2.70
25	2.56
26	2.44
27	2.32
28	2.21
29	2.11
30	2.02
31	1.94
32	1.86
33	1.79
34	1.72
35	1.66
36	1.60
37	1.54
38	1.49

Mean Water Temp to Air Temp DT (°C)	Correction Factor
39	1.44
40	1.39
41	1.35
42	1.31
43	1.27
44	1.23
45	1.19
46	1.16
47	1.13
48	1.10
49	1.07

This is a continuation of the table from the previous page

Hydraulic Separation

Hydraulic separation uses the science, **water will always find the easiest route**. If we have 2 different flow rates required on a system we can separate these with some form of hydraulic separation, we are essentially splitting the system into smaller independent systems.

Hydraulic separation is frequently used on commercial systems and larger domestic systems and can come in different forms. The most common ways of installing hydraulic separation are via a low loss header (LLH), a buffer tank, plate heat exchangers and close-coupling of the flow and return pipes (CCT'S).

Reasons for installing separation

One common reason for installing separation is if **multiple pumps** are required on a system. It is not recommended to install pumps in 'series' as they will often fight against one another when determining their flow rates however if we were to separate these pumps then they can pump around their 'own' part of the system under their own flow rates and not affect the other pump. This is particularly useful if an appliance has an integral pump, but this isn't capable of overcoming the resistance of the system, a second pump can be installed after some form of separation to cope with the demand required for the system. Also, if a **differing Delta T** is required on different zones of the system, then separation could provide this option.

Plate Heat Exchangers

Plate heat exchangers differ from the other forms of separation as they **physically** separate the two systems, this is useful in a number of scenarios such as having **differing pressures** on systems or even **differing fluids.** Their potential disadvantage that must be considered by engineers is that they do restrict the flow rate considerably.

Close-Coupled Tees

If the flow and return are piped in **close proximity** to one another on a system, then the flow of water will choose to move down the flow and directly up the return rather than to the system. This would then provide the option for the engineer to install a second pump onto the system to deal with the emitters whilst still extracting heat from the appliance. As shown below:

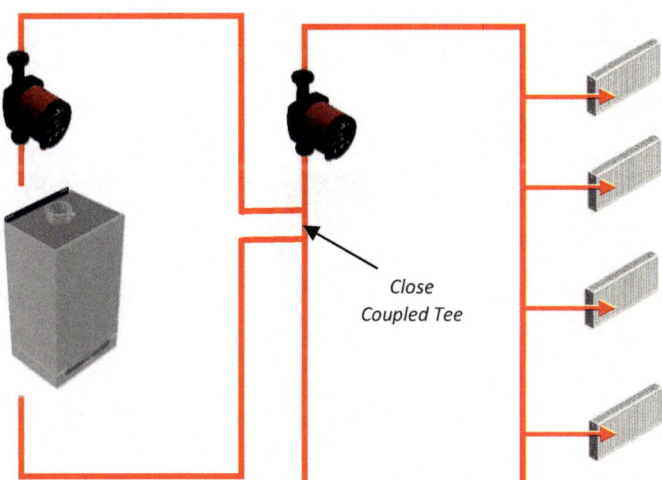

*Close
Coupled Tee*

Buffers and Low Loss Headers

The science behind a buffer tank or a low loss header is that
they are essentially a large body of water, think of these as just
a piece of pipework with a huge diameter. As the volume is so
large inside these components the water entering them is
essentially not being 'pushed' through the system with any
force at this point. (velocity will be discussed on page 68).
Imagine if you ran a 15mm pipe into a large swimming pool –
once the water from the pipe enters the pool it is now just
'floating' around under no pressure. This is why you will often
find some Low Loss Headers (LLH's) with built in dirt and air
separators, any air entering will have the chance to rise up and
any dirt can now fall and settle. This is the same reason that
radiators often attract air and sludge, they also have a larger
volume inside than the pipework feeding them.

Once the water is in the Buffer or LLH we can then extract it
under a different flow rate by installing a pump on the other
side to where the water entered the Buffer/LLH. Having a flow
and return on both 'sides' of the Buffer or LLH will mean that
we now have two separate circuits essentially using the same
water but flowing at different speeds.

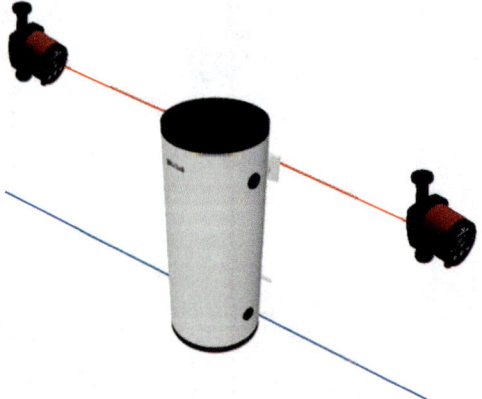

Buffers with Heat Pumps

Primarily to aid with **defrost cycles,** manufacturers will state a minimum **volume** of **constant water** within the system e.g. 40 Litres. A defrost cycle is when a heat pump essentially turns into an air conditioning unit and **reverses** its usual operation by taking heat out of the property and places it outside, this heat now enables any frost to melt on the outdoor unit. Usually, manufacturers will also state that the water content within the heat pump cannot be added to this calculation nor can any radiators featuring TRV's or heating areas that are zoned. Due to the volume of water within buffer tanks they *can* be used as a means of adding this required volume to a system, but we will explore the potential disadvantages of this on page 59.

The circulating Pump inside of most modern Heat Pumps is a pulse width modulation pump (PWM) this essentially means that it is in direct communication with the Heat Pump and most are attempting to maintain a **DT of 5°C.**

If a buffer tank is fitted to a system the benefit to the heat pump is that it should, in theory, always be capable of achieving a DT of 5°C no matter what is happening with the system itself. Water will always find the easiest route so if this means that it will be traveling through the buffer down the return and back to the heat pump this is what will happen.

We could potentially have a situation where the flow rate is severely reduced on the emitter circuit as a result of zones turning off or TRV's reducing down the flow, but the heat pump's circulating pump will still be attempting to maintain a DT of 5°C for as long a period as possible.

If a buffer tank is to be used within a system, then we must ensure that both 'sides' of the separation operate at a similar flow rate to each other for as long a period as possible. If the flow rates are equal, then the majority of the flow of water will be straight through the buffer tank as this will be the 'easiest' route. This is shown in the image at the bottom of the page here.

Methods of achieving the desired flow rates is covered later in this book and involves calculating the correct pipe size, the correct pump size/setting and the correct use of controls.

Engineers must be aware that installing a buffer tank will negatively affect the efficiency of some systems and so the decision to install one should be taken within a full design calculation and not as the first action if an engineer is attempting to install the most efficient system as possible.

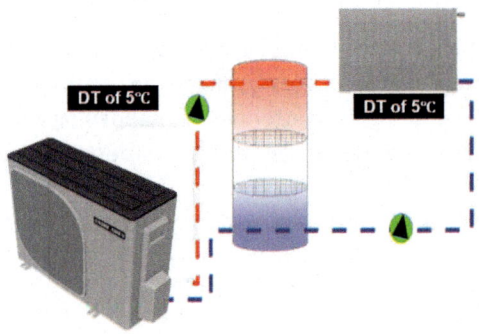

Disadvantages of Separation

It's easy to move away from logic when delving into the depths of heating system design so the most important point to remember in all of this is, **the heat from our appliance should go into our emitters**. If we place a large volume of water such as buffer between our emitters and the heat source, then we have already lost some efficiency. If we have a scenario such as in the image below where the emitter system is constantly at a differing flow rate than the heat pump's flow rate then this is exacerbated and the efficiency drops even further, the technical name for this is **distortion**. Distortion ultimately causes the appliance to run at a higher flow temperature than if separation was not installed. The key point with buffer tanks is that they should never be used to compensate for a lack of system design. A good understanding of their function and their advantages and disadvantages will allow a heating engineer to decide whether one is needed on an install or not.

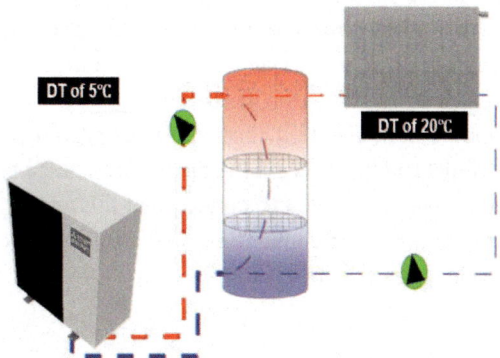

One final point to make is that if a buffer tank is to be installed on a system this **must only be on the emitter circuit** and not the hot water circuit. On a D plan system, the flow from the heat pump would go to a diverter valve where it will be sent to either the hot water circuit **or** the buffer tank, the emitters would then be piped from the buffer.

Open loop systems

When designing a heat pump system, in most cases the most efficient way to install this would be something referred to as an 'open loop system'. This has been proven by research data. An open loop system is nothing fancy, in fact it is the opposite, it is keeping the system as simple as possible in order to get the heat created within the heat pump into the property as quickly and easily as possible and to also ensure the heat pump 'cycles' as little as possible. Zone valves, TRV's and on/off thermostats are all components that were created to stop too much heat entering a property or space. They are all versions of a temperature limiter **not a modulation of temperature.** These devices will cause excess cycling of a heat pump and therefore potentially a reduction in efficiency. There is an issue with 'open loop systems' in that some aspects of it can be argued contradict the 'guidance' offered by Part L. Installers, designers and developers need to be aware of this when carrying out their work and **make their own informed decision** on if they will install a full open loop system.

Pipe Sizing Calculations

Mass Flow Rate

Mass flow rate is the foundation for everything within heating system design and can be used to understand a range of principles that a heating engineer will experience every day. There is a useful calculation tool to determine the relationship flow rate has with the other factors within the system and this is called the **Mass flow rate triangle.**

The triangle works on the premise that kW is related to both the flow rate, the Delta-T and the substance's specific heat capacity (SHC) within the system. This calculation triangle is similar to the Ohms law triangle within electrics, you cover the value you want to calculate, and the sum is what is left from the triangle.

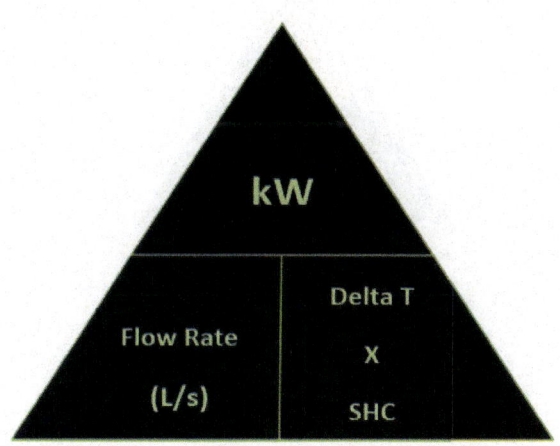

For example, if I wanted to find the **flow rate** (L/s) I would cover this value up. As you can see below the calculation is;

Flow Rate = kW ÷ (DT X SHC)

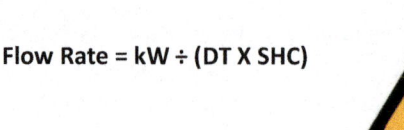

Similarly, if we were to calculate the kW, this value would be covered up and as flow rate (L/s) and DT x SHC are next to each other we multiply these. The calculation would therefore be;

kW = Flow Rate x (DT x SHC)

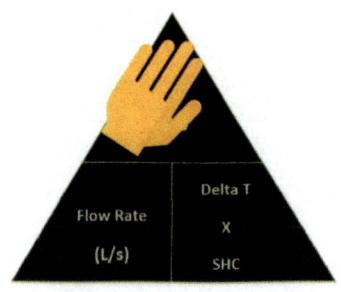

Specific Heat Capacity

Specific Heat Capacity (SHC) was briefly touched upon at the start of this book, it is essentially a measurement of how much energy is required to raise the temperature of a substance by 1°C (or 1 Kelvin) and once this temperature is raised the energy used to do so is 'held' within the substance, this is an important fact to remember.

Fresh water has a SHC of 4.18kj, however, for any future calculations we will round this to **4.2kj** for the ease of arithmetic.

If you were to add salt to a pan of water you would change its SHC from 4.2kj to around 3.9kj, this therefore means that the pan of salt water would not require as much heat energy to reach 100°C as a pan of fresh water would, hence the reason that adding salt speeds up the boiling process when cooking.

The Effect of Glycol

Many heat pump manufacturers of monobloc units will state that a method of protecting the heat pump from freezing in a power outage will need to be installed in order to maintain warranty. Modern heat pumps will sense their primary water getting to a low temperature and automatically create heat to prevent this but if the power is out then this would not be possible. In reality the risk of this happening is quite low.

The installer has two options if they wish to adhere to the manufacturers guidance, one is to install an **Anti-Freeze Valve** onto the outdoor pipework at the lowest level of the system. These valves sense the temperature of the water inside them and if this is at a critically low point they will automatically open up and deposit the water from the heat pump, drop the pressure within and therefore prevent the risk of the heat pump's components freezing. The other option would be to add **Glycol** to the system (a form of anti-freeze) this however has a detrimental impact on performance as it effects the specific heat capacity.

One number a heat pump system designer can remember to make their tasks quicker is **21**. This is the number that will fill the bottom right corner of the mass flow rate triangle on every occasion if the system **does not** contain glycol and has been designed to a Delta T of 5°C.

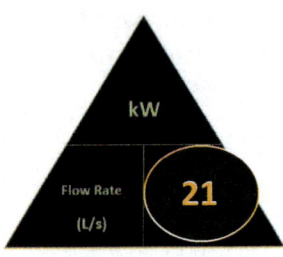

Heat Pump – no glycol

(5 x 4.2 = 21)

However as stated previously, if we were to add a glycol mix the the SHC of the water within the system will be altered, a 25% glycol to 75% water mix is common within UK systems and this ratio drops the SHC of the water down to 3.8kj. This therfore changes the bottom right corner to **19.**

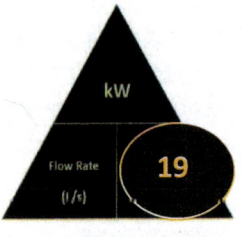

25% Glycol mix

Using this information, we can now calculate the effect that a 25% glycol mix has on the maximum heat output of a heat pump.

As an example, we will say that the system is running at 0.47 L/s. Now, using the mass flow rate triangle we can determine the maximum kW we can achieve with this flow rate.

- No glycol system = 0.47 x **21** = **9.87kW**
- 25% glycol mix system = 0.47 x **19** = **8.93kW**

As the results show, almost a kW of heat is potentially lost from the maximum output. This is another factor that an engineer designing a heat pump system must consider.

Condensing Boilers

An engineer designing a system with a condensing boiler may wish to remember the number **84.** Again, following the pattern previously stated, this is the result of the Delta T now changing to 20°C and the water of course containing no glycol, so the SHC is 4.2.

(20 x 4.2 = 84)

The mass flow rate triangle can be used in a number of instances. Most gas engineers will know that a 30kW combination boiler will heat the incoming cold mains by 35°C if the flow rate at the tap is 12 litres per minute. This is a generic guidance for all manufacturers whose boiler has a plate heat exchanger, the reason for this is because it is science. We can place these numbers into the triangle and see that it would be scientifically and mathematically impossible for a manufacturer to better this result.

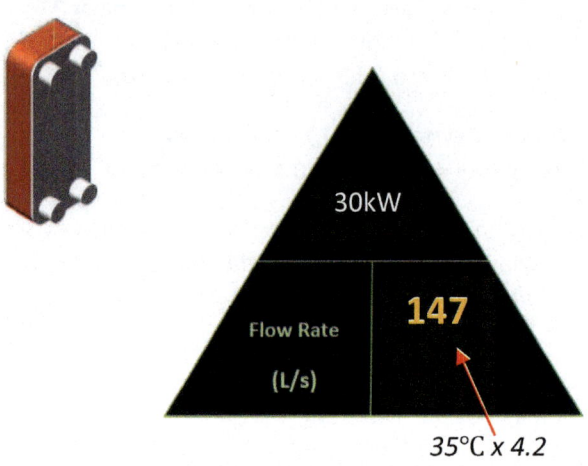

As you can see we have inputted the size of the appliance (30kW) and the calculation for our DT x SHC into the triangle (35 x 4.2 = 147).

Now, to calculate how fast we can run the tap to achieve this temperature increase, we simply divide 30 by 147.

30 ÷ 147 = 0.20 L/s (x 60 = 12Litres per minute)

Pipe Sizing

Selecting the correct pipe size for a heating installation is one of the most important aspects of design. Over the years a 'rule of thumb' approach has begun to creep into some installations, and this has caused issues with performance and efficiency of a range of heating appliances be them heat pumps, gas boilers or others.

When selecting a suitable pipe size for a section of the heating system we must use the **Mass flow rate triangle**.

Using the triangle will enable us to select a **suitable size (diameter)** of pipe that is capable of delivering the;

- **Required heat (in kW)** to the various areas of the system.

- We must also ensure that the water is travelling fast enough **(velocity)** to reach the target and not allow sludge to settle but not too fast that it causes noise.

- We must finally calculate that the **restrictions** caused by the pipe diameter and any fittings can be overcome by the power **(head) of our circulating pump**.

Step 1 is to find the kW required per section of pipework in the system. As shown in the diagram below, pipework **section A** will need to be capable of 'carrying' **2kW** worth of heat energy as it is supplying the two radiators, however pipework **section B** will only be required to supply **1kW** as it is solely connected to one radiator.

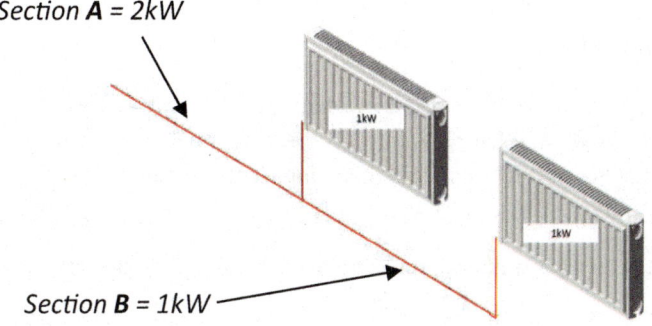

*Section **A** = 2kW*

*Section **B** = 1kW*

Step 2 is to now calculate the flow rate required for a section of pipework using the mass flow rate triangle. We will use pipework **section A** from the diagram as our example and we will install a heat pump with no glycol in the system (therefore our DT is 5°C and our SHC is 4.2).

Section A flow rate required;

$$2kW \div (5 \times 4.2) = 0.095 \text{ L/s}$$

Step 3 now involves choosing a **provisional** pipe size based upon the flow rate we have previously calculated. For this book we will use the reference charts starting on **page 80** for this task (there are other reference charts available). When you turn to the reference charts you will see that the tables are split into the individual diameters of pipe. (10mm – 35mm) It is important to note that these are all in reference to copper pipework and not plastic.

There are 3 columns within the table stating;

Loss per metre (mm), Flow Rate (L/s) and Velocity (M/s)

Velocity (m/s)

To decide which diameter is most suitable (for now) we select this based on **Velocity.** Velocity is the speed in which the water is flowing through the pipe, this is measured in metres per second (m/s).

It is recommended that the velocity is as close to 0.9m/s as possible.

The velocity can be **as low as 0.5 m/s** however, anything below this will result in a **build-up of sediment** in the system as the water will not be flowing quickly enough to dislodge this.

The maximum could potentially be as high as **1.5 m/s**, however it is recommended that anything **over 1 m/s** will begin to create 'noise' especially within components such as radiator valves so the charts within this book are limited to 1m/s.

Selecting a Provisional Pipe Size

As previously stated, the pipe size is selected based on velocity in the first instance, and as the optimum velocity is 0.9 m/s then the pipe size should be selected based upon which diameter allows our calculated flow rate to provide as close as possible to this **0.9 m/s**.

For our example we will again use the **section A** pipework in our first example of **2kW** and a flow rate of **0.095 L/s.** We now scroll through the pipe size charts and select a suitable size of pipe based upon this, if the exact L/s is not in the chart (which is likely) then the closest value above this should be used, in this example **0.096 L/s**. Based upon velocity, only **15mm pipe** would be suitable in this example so is chosen as our provisional pipe size, if there were multiple pipe sizes that could be used then the one allowing a velocity as close to 0.9 m/s should be selected.

15mm Copper Pipe

Loss per Metre	Flow Rate	Velocity
28	0.07	0.5
30	0.073	0.5
32	0.076	0.5
35	0.08	0.5
37	0.082	0.5
40	0.085	0.6
41	0.088	0.6
44	0.091	0.6
46	0.094	0.6
49	0.096	0.6
51	0.099	0.7
53	0.101	0.7
55	0.104	0.7
58	0.106	0.7
60	0.108	0.7

Loss per Metre (Resistance)

The final aspect of choosing a suitable pipework diameter that we must consider is the **resistance** that is created by the pipework and the fittings used. The first column in the charts gives the pressure loss per metre of straight pipe. This data becomes vitally important when selecting and setting a circulating pump and so should be noted down as this stage.

Again, referring to the chart and the flow rate we have just calculated, we can see that with a flow rate of **0.096 L/s** and a velocity of **0.6 m/s** the pressure loss per metre in this pipe would be **49mm.**

You now of course multiply this value by the length of the pipework in that section to find the total pressure loss in that section. It is normally accepted that both flow and return are similar lengths and so the length can be calculated from this. For our example we will use **10m** of pipework in this section so therefore the total **pipework** loss for section A is **490mm.**

15mm Copper Pipe

Loss per Metre	Flow Rate	Velocity
28	0.07	0.5
30	0.073	0.5
32	0.076	0.5
35	0.08	0.5
37	0.082	0.5
40	0.085	0.6
41	0.088	0.6
44	0.091	0.6
46	0.094	0.6
49	0.096	0.6
51	0.099	0.7
53	0.101	0.7
55	0.104	0.7
58	0.106	0.7
60	0.108	0.7

Resistance of Fittings

Within the calculation of our system's resistance, we must also consider the pressure loss across any radiators, fittings and any other components that will be installed on the pipework too.

Manufacturers of these components can give the individual resistance for each but in a large system calculating this can be quite time consuming. Examples of this would be that a radiator would add 1 metre of resistance per 1 metre of radiator width or a single 15mm press fit elbow would add 1.4 metres.

The 'Quicker' Method

It is generally accepted that the engineer can add between **33% and 50%** pressure loss to the pipework resistance value to account for these fittings and components on the system.

So, in our example we will add **40%** to our **490mm** pipework resistance;

$$490 \times 1.4 \ (40\%) = 686mm$$

To add 33% simply multiply by 1.33.

-

To add 50%, simply multiply by 1.5.

Recording Information

Over the previous pages we have calculated a number of pieces of data that must be referred to for the next stages of the design. Therefore, it is imperative that this information is recorded in a clear and efficient manner.

Section	Pipe Size (mm)	kW	Flow Rate (L/s)	Velocity (m/s)	Total Resistance (mm per m)
A	15	2	0.095	0.6	686
B	10	1	0.047	0.8	625
C	22	5	0.238	0.7	555
D	28	10	0.47	0.9	592

Above is an example of how this data could be laid out for ease of reference during a design. It is important to note that at this stage of the process the pipe size chosen is still provisional and so this data could change, therefore a digital version is ideal if any alterations need to be made further down the line.

One note of interest within the table above is the 'total resistance' column. Ideally, the resistances within this column should be roughly of a similar unit. As water will always find it's easiest route, if a resistance was extremely lower in one section than others, we may end up with this section almost 'stealing' the flow from the rest of the system. When an engineer balances radiators, they are technically just increasing the resistance to prevent this.

Calculating the Index Circuit

The final stage relating to pipe sizing is to calculate how much 'power' we need from our circulating pump to overcome the resistances in our pipework sections that we have recorded previously. To do this we must calculate the **index circuit**. The index circuit is the route of pipework from the heat source to a radiator that **has the highest resistance**. It is **not the sum** of all the resistances.

The calculation for this task is as follows, starting at the heat source and with an end point of each radiator in the system we must add together the resistance of each section of pipework we travel down and record this number. The route with the highest resistance is the index circuit. The index circuit is not always the furthest radiator away from the heat source as pipe size, fittings, length of run and components can all influence the resistance of a route so all must be calculated.

An example of how to record this data is shown below, the route **to Lounge** is the index circuit in this scenario.

Route	Total Resistance
Heat Pump to **Kitchen**	1948.8mm
Heat Pump to **Lounge**	2354.8mm
Heat Pump to **Hall**	1990.4mm
Heat Pump to **Bathroom**	1890.8mm
Heat Pump to **Bed 1**	2116mm
Heat Pump to **Bed 2**	2022mm

Cylinder Coil Resistance

The resistance within a domestic hot water cylinder's coil can be found from most manufacturers, it is however unlikely that this resistance would be higher than a typical radiator circuit within a property that contains a 'regular sized' heating circuit and therefore unlikely to be found as the index circuit but can still be calculated to confirm.

Heating Appliance Resistance

Every heating appliance will have a resistance as the water passes through the heat exchanger and this data is available from most manufacturers. This resistance must now be added to the index circuit in our example this was **2354.8mm** but for ease of calculations we will convert to **2.35 metres**. It must be noted that certain magnetic filters/strainers will also have a resistance value, and this again can be found through most manufacturers.

We will state in our example that our heat pump's heat exchanger has a resistance of **1.2 metres** and the magnetic filter has a resistance of **0.28 metres.**

So, the total resistance of the index circuit is now:

1.2m + 0.28m + 2.35m = **3.83m of resistance**

Confirming Pipe Sizes

It is at this stage that the pipe size diameters we provisionally selected for each section can be finalised or altered if necessary. If the appliance we have selected to install has an integral pump, then the maximum head of pressure it can produce must be capable of overcoming the index circuit's resistance. If it cannot then we may need to assess whether a larger diameter of pipework will need to be selected for a particular section of the system to reduce the resistance of the index circuit (this will have a detrimental effect on velocity however). The alternative option we have in this scenario is to install a second pump, but this would need to be hydraulically separated from the integral pump.

If we are installing a circulator pump (e.g. for a heat only boiler) then this selection of size will be based using the data collected by calculating the index circuit.

In our example, we will have a Wilo Para 15/8 integral pump, this means that we have up to **8 metres of potential head pressure**. As we have up to 8 metres of pressure but we only have **3.83 metres** of resistance we will need to lower the output of the pump to maximise the efficiency.

Setting Pumps

To adjust the setting of the pump speed to suit the system we have designed we must refer to the individual pump chart as seen below. As this is a PWM pump we can select a suitable modulation 'curve' based on the maximum pressure that will need to be produced for our particular system. For this we must find our **'Duty Point'**.

Firstly, we take the **maximum flow rate** that our system will need to produce. In this example 10kW is the maximum. Therefore, using the mass flow rate triangle we will need **0.47 litres per second (10÷ (5x4.2))** and draw a vertical line at this reading on the chart (this is shown as the **vertical yellow** line). Next, we must draw a horizontal line at the total resistance of the index circuit we calculated previously, **3.83 metres**, (this is shown as the **horizontal yellow** line below). The duty point is the area that these two lines **cross**, as this is between 65% and 75% on our chart then **75%** must be selected in the control menu.

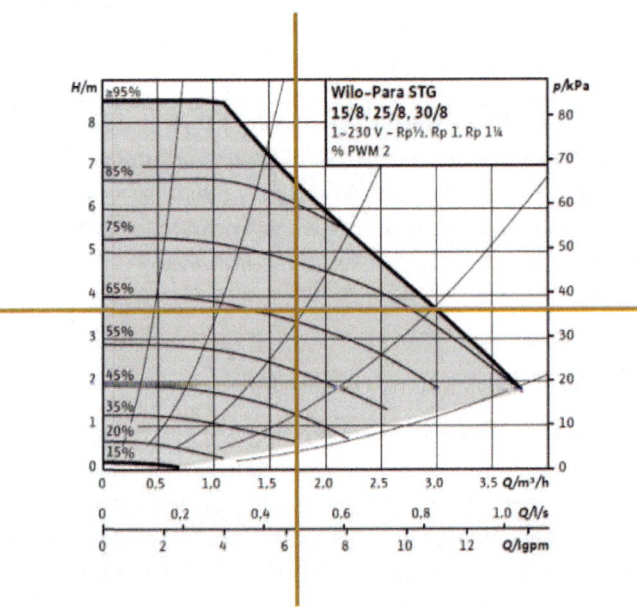

10mm Copper Pipe

Loss per Metre	Flow Rate	Velocity
53	0.029	0.5
55	0.0298	0.5
58	0.0305	0.5
60	0.0312	0.5
63	0.032	0.5
64	0.0326	0.5
67	0.0332	0.6
69	0.0339	0.6
72	0.0345	0.6
74	0.0351	0.6
76	0.0358	0.6
79	0.0364	0.6
81	0.037	0.6
83	0.0377	0.6
86	0.0382	0.6
88	0.0388	0.6
90	0.0394	0.7
93	0.04	0.7
95	0.0406	0.7
98	0.0411	0.7
99	0.0417	0.7
102	0.0423	0.7
104	0.0429	0.7
107	0.0433	0.7
109	0.0439	0.7
111	0.0445	0.7
113	0.0445	0.7
116	0.0455	0.8
118	0.0456	0.8
121	0.0465	0.8
122	0.0469	0.8
125	0.0474	0.8
127	0.0479	0.8
130	0.0484	0.8
132	0.0488	0.8
134	0.0489	0.8
136	0.0502	0.8
139	0.0523	0.8
150	0.0548	0.9
162	0.0568	0.9

Loss per Metre	Flow Rate	Velocity
174	0.0588	0.9
185	0.0608	1
197	0.0628	1
208	0.0648	1

This is a continuation of the 10mm copper table from the previous page

15mm Copper Pipe

Loss per Metre	Flow Rate	Velocity
28	0.07	0.5
30	0.073	0.5
32	0.076	0.5
35	0.08	0.5
37	0.082	0.5
40	0.085	0.6
41	0.088	0.6
44	0.091	0.6
46	0.094	0.6
49	0.096	0.6
51	0.099	0.7
53	0.101	0.7
55	0.104	0.7
58	0.106	0.7
60	0.108	0.7
63	0.111	0.7
64	0.113	0.8
67	0.115	0.8
69	0.117	0.8
72	0.12	0.8
74	0.122	0.8
76	0.124	0.8
79	0.126	0.8
81	0.128	0.9
83	0.13	0.9
86	0.132	0.9
88	0.134	0.9
90	0.136	0.9

Loss per Metre	Flow Rate	Velocity
93	0.138	0.9
95	0.14	0.9
98	0.142	0.9
99	0.144	1
102	0.146	1
104	0.148	1
107	0.149	1
109	0.151	1
111	0.153	1
113	0.155	1
116	0.156	1

This is a continuation of the 15mm copper table from the previous page

22mm Copper Pipe

Loss per Metre	Flow Rate	Velocity
15	0.144	0.5
17	0.15	0.5
17	0.156	0.5
18	0.161	0.5
20	0.167	0.5
21	0.172	0.5
22	0.178	0.6
23	0.183	0.6
24	0.188	0.6
26	0.193	0.6
28	0.203	0.6
30	0.212	0.7
32	0.221	0.7
35	0.23	0.7
37	0.238	0.7
40	0.247	0.8
41	0.255	0.8
44	0.263	0.8
46	0.27	0.8
49	0.278	0.9
51	0.286	0.9
53	0.293	0.9
55	0.3	0.9
58	0.307	1
60	0.314	1
63	0.321	1
64	0.328	1
67	0.334	1

28mm Copper Pipe

Loss per Metre	Flow Rate	Velocity
12	0.25	0.5
12	0.263	0.5
14	0.277	0.5
15	0.289	0.5
17	0.302	0.6
17	0.314	0.6
18	0.325	0.6
20	0.336	0.6
21	0.348	0.6
22	0.359	0.7
23	0.369	0.7
24	0.38	0.7
26	0.39	0.7
28	0.408	0.8
30	0.428	0.8
32	0.446	0.8
35	0.464	0.9
37	0.482	0.9
40	0.5	0.9
41	0.518	1
44	0.533	1

35mm Copper Pipe

Loss per Metre	Flow Rate	Velocity
8	0.4	0.5
9	0.424	0.5
10	0.448	0.5
11	0.475	0.6
12	0.499	0.6
13	0.523	0.6
14	0.543	0.7
15	0.564	0.7
16	0.604	0.7
17	0.623	0.7
18	0.645	0.8
19	0.669	0.8
20	0.686	0.8
21	0.704	0.8
22	0.735	0.9
24	0.773	0.9
26	0.805	1
28	0.838	1
30	0.869	1

Summary

I do hope that this book has provided the reader with a clearer understanding of heating system design. Whether an engineer goes on to utilise this knowledge is completely up to them but at least having the tools in the arsenal is an advantage.

This may inspire some installers to stop paying a system design engineer and attempt their own designs in future. It may encourage some engineers to completely 'down tools' and become designers themselves full time. Alternatively, it may completely put some people off designing and that's fine too, at least they now have the knowledge to make that decision for themselves.

You may have noticed that I never referred to the 'gas industry' or the 'heat pump industry' in this publication. To me we are the **'heating industry'** and I want to encourage more engineers into this sector, whether they choose to install gas boilers or heat pumps is essentially up to their customers. I personally would love to see the next generation of engineers being capable and confident of designing, installing, commissioning, and repairing a range of systems no matter the heat source, as that would mean greater job opportunities and job security.

There has never been a more exciting time to be a part of this industry, whatever is happening now or will happen in the future, one thing is certain, we are definitely not standing still and how interesting and exciting is that to be a part of moving forward.

Printed in Great Britain
by Amazon